JOHN MAXWELL

150

ESSENTIAL INSIGHTS ON

LEADERSHIP

HARVEST HOUSE PUBLISHERS
EUGENE, OREGON

Scripture quotations are taken from the Holman Christian Standard Bible®, Copyright © 1999, 2000, 2002, 2003, 2009 by Holman Bible Publishers. Used by permission. Holman Christian Standard Bible®, Holman CSB®, and HCSB® are federally registered trademarks of Holman Bible Publishers.

Cover design by Bryce Williamson

Cover photo © venimo / Gettyimages

Interior design by Chad Dougherty

Content development by Meadow's Edge Group LLC

Includes material from these sources:

John C. Maxwell, *The Right to Lead* (Simple Truths, 2009). www.simpletruths.com. Used by permission.

John C. Maxwell, *Own Your Dreams* (Simple Truths / SUCCESS Books, 2009, 2012). www.simple truths.com. All rights reserved. Used by permission.

Zig Ziglar, *Inspiration 365 Days a Year* (Simple Truths, 2008). www.simpletruths.com. All rights reserved. Used by permission.

Other quotes were gleaned from John Maxwell speeches delivered at the annual convention of the Christian Booksellers Association.

150 Essential Insights on Leadership
Copyright © 2014 by Meadows Edge Group LLC
Published by Harvest House Publishers
Eugene, Oregon 97408
www.harvesthousepublishers.com

ISBN 978-0-7369-8212-2 (pbk.)
ISBN 978-0-7369-8416-4 (hardcover)
ISBN 978-0-7369-8213-9 (eBook)

Printed in the United States of America

20 21 22 23 24 25 26 27 28 / VP-CD / 10 9 8 7 6 5 4 3 2 1

The one who looks intently into the perfect law of freedom and perseveres in it, and is not a forgetful hearer but one who does good works— this person will be blessed in what he does.

JAMES 1:25

*Everything begins with a decision.
Then we have to manage that decision
for the rest of our lives.*

CONTENTS

INTRODUCTION

John C. Maxwell is one of those rare individuals with a pastor's gracious heart and a businessperson's keen mind.

Maxwell, the son of a pastor, followed in his father's footsteps. For a quarter of a century, he pastored churches in Indiana, California, and Florida. He then embarked on a second career as an internationally respected leadership expert.

He has written more than 70 books with sales of more than 20 million copies. Some have been million-copy best-sellers, including *Developing the Leader Within You, The 21 Irrefutable Laws of Leadership,* and *The 21 Indispensable Qualities of a Leader.* He was one of 25 authors named to Amazon.com's Tenth Anniversary Hall of Fame.

He has worked as a leadership trainer and consultant with the United States Military Academy, the National

7

Basketball Association, the National Football League, and the United Nations. He speaks to more than 350,000 people each year. He is also the founder of EQUIP Leadership, Inc., a nonprofit company that has trained more than 5 million leaders in 126 countries around the world.

Maxwell's website is JohnMaxwell.com.

DREAM WITH VISION

Now to Him who is able to do above and beyond all that we ask or think according to the power that works in us—to Him be glory in the church and in Christ Jesus to all generations, forever and ever. Amen.

EPHESIANS 3:20-21

Dreams are **VALUABLE** commodities. They propel us forward. They give us energy. They make us **ENTHUSIASTIC**. Everyone ought to have a dream.

You may have never thought of your dreams as children, but that's what they are. They are your offspring—the **JOY** of your today and the hope of your future. Protect them. Feed them. Nurture them. Encourage them to grow.

A genuine dream
is a picture and a blueprint
of a person's **PURPOSE**
and **POTENTIAL**.

Your vision must be **BIGGER** than you. The greater it is, the more resources it will require. The **BEST** leaders bring all of the resources in their world into play to accomplish something **GREAT**.

If your dream is really **YOUR** dream, then it will seem **OUTRAGEOUS** to more than a few people.

You may have many dreams. Yet there must be one that **STANDS OUT** above all the others...one that inspires you, energizes you, and empowers you to do everything you can to **ACHIEVE** it.

The reason most people never realize their dreams is that they have no **STRATEGY** in place for attaining them. They have no knowledge of what is needed and what must sometimes be **SACRIFICED** to have the dream come **TRUE**.

You can't borrow somebody else's **VISION**. It must come from **INSIDE** of you.

All **EFFECTIVE** leaders have a vision of what they must accomplish. That vision becomes the **ENERGY** behind every effort and the **FORCE** that pushes through all the problems. With vision, a leader is on a **MISSION**. His or her contagious spirit is felt among the crowd until others begin to rise alongside.

No vision is worthy of your life unless it **FULFILLS** your destiny, the purpose for which you were designed. Your vision must contribute to your **DESTINY**.

You can't reach for a **DREAM** and remain safely mediocre at the same time. The two are **INCOMPATIBLE**.

Albert Einstein, a dreamer and thinker, understood the value of the **IMAGINATION**. He called his imagination a "**HOLY CURIOSITY**."

If you come from a discouraging background, or you don't think of yourself as an especially imaginative person, don't lose hope. You can still **DISCOVER** and **DEVELOP** a dream. God has put that ability in every one of us.

When you **OWN** your dream, it will feel right on you. It will provide **WINGS** to your spirit. You will feel you were made to do it.

Successful people—those who see and **SEIZE** their dream—love what they do and do what they **LOVE**.

God designs us to want to do what we are most **CAPABLE** of doing. Because of this, when we do things that are making an impact, something **RESONATES** within us.

Success isn't an event—
it's a **LIFESTYLE**. Dreams are
fulfilled when someone
performs with **EXCELLENCE**
day after day.

It's never too late
to start **DREAMING** and
PURSUING your dreams.

Learn to say no to the **GOOD** so you can say yes to the **BEST**.

BEGIN WELL TO END WELL

*I am sure of this, that He who
started a good work in you
will carry it on to completion
until the day of Christ Jesus.*

PHILIPPIANS 1:6

Only a **CLEAR PICTURE** of who you are and where you want to go can help you **PRIORITIZE** what you need to do. We all make choices. Clarity of **VISION** creates clarity of **PRIORITIES**.

In the beginning, you just need to get **MOVING**. Try different things. It's much easier to start doing something **RIGHT** if you've already started doing **SOMETHING**.

The **TIMING** will never be perfect for you to pursue your dream, so you might as well start **NOW**.

Give God the first part of every **DAY**.
Give God the first day of every **WEEK**.
Give God the first portion of your **INCOME**.
Give God the first consideration in every **DECISION**.
Give God the first place in your **LIFE**.

Most people have no idea how to **ACHIEVE** their dreams. What they possess is a **VAGUE NOTION** that there is something they would like to do someday or someone they would like to become. But they don't know how to get from **HERE** to **THERE**.

If you want to **CHANGE** and **GROW**, then you must know yourself and accept who you are before you can start **BUILDING**.

A good student of
LEADERSHIP
can learn lessons almost
ANYWHERE.

The more **DEFINED** you are in your pursuit of daily disciplines, the greater **CLARITY** you have on the things you should or should not do. Andy Stanley, author of *Visioneering*, says, "Clarity of Vision is more important than Certainty of the Outcome."

When you become clear on what you do each day, you will see the **OUTCOMES** that you desire—many times and much **SOONER** than you anticipated.

BE A DOER AS WELL AS A DREAMER

There is profit in all hard work,
but endless talk leads only to poverty.

PROVERBS 14:23

We cannot **ACHIEVE** our wildest dreams by **REMAINING** who we are.

RESULTS matter. What good is a masterfully planned **STRATEGY** that doesn't yield **POSITIVE** results?

No one wants to feel **INVISIBLE** as they pass through life, yet we often get the impression that others see us as little more than a **STATISTIC**. Our résumé ends up in a pile, our performance reviews go into a file, and like everyone else, we get a raise every once in a while. We're referred to as applicants, employees, or human resources, and we sense our individuality being somewhat **BURIED...**

…Most people go with the flow, doing what's asked of them but not much more. The key to **ELEVATING** yourself in business is to go above and beyond **EXPECTATIONS** whenever you're asked a question or given an assignment.

Daydreamers have dreams that are merely **DISTRACTIONS** from their current work.

The basis of **COURAGE** is individual **INITIATIVE**. If we cannot act alone, we cannot act together.

Show me a man who cannot bother to do **LITTLE THINGS**, and I'll show you a man who cannot be trusted to do **BIG THINGS**.

Uncommon leaders are **ACTIVISTS**: They are doers, and they **EMPOWER** others by their actions.

No **ADVICE**

on **SUCCESS** works

unless you do.

Uncommon leaders are **INDUSTRIALISTS**: They roll up their sleeves and work **HARD**.

The **FEAR** of rejection or failure creates **INACTION**.

You will have to **GIVE UP** things to achieve your dreams. And the greatest challenge isn't giving up the obvious things that will hurt you. It will be giving up the **GOOD THINGS** that you like, but that won't help you.

Men and women who lead on the highest level are quite **EXTRAORDINARY**. They are people of **ACTION** who have their **PRIORITIES** in line.

What is it that drives **GROWTH?** As important as it is have a growth mindset, I believe growth is a **BYPRODUCT** or outcome of a series of **INTENTIONAL PRACTICES** that leaders and teams do as a part of their daily routine...If you keep **LEARNING** and **GROWING** every day over the course of many years, you will be astounded by how far it will take you.

What a person knows at **FIFTY** that he did not know at twenty is not the knowledge of formulas or forms of words, but of people, places, actions—**KNOWLEDGE** gained by touch, sight, sound, victories, failures, sleeplessness, devotion, love. He knows the human **EXPERIENCES** and **EMOTIONS** of this earth, and of oneself and of other people.

If you have dreams, goals, or aspirations, you need to **GROW** to achieve them. But if you're like I was—and if you are like most people—you have one or more mistaken beliefs that create a gap that keeps you from growing and **REACHING** your potential. Each of us has the opportunity to bridge that gap. But we must make that a **GOAL** and follow through.

COURAGE teaches us what should be feared and what ought not to be feared. Only by taking **ACTION** do we gain that knowledge.

Imagine that you have a **DECISION** to make, but you just aren't sure about it. So you put it off. Sometimes that's a wise move because the timing isn't right. *When* to lead is as important as what to do and where to go. I believe that **TIMING** plays a critical role in many of the decisions we make. **WAITING** to act can be a wise decision. We might need more information, or perhaps the people who will be affected need to be prepared. But when you wait, are you always practicing good timing? Or do you put things off unnecessarily? In those cases, maybe you're **PROCRASTINATING**.

Our **POTENTIAL**
is God's gift to us,
and what we do with it
is our gift to **HIM**.

Choosing to **LEAD** your life
and not just accept it
is critical to **OWNING**
your dream.

Leadership
is a **CHOICE** you make,
not a **PLACE** you sit.

You will never **CHANGE** your life until you change something you do daily. The secret of your **SUCCESS** is found in your **DAILY ROUTINE**.

You never **REGAIN** lost time, so make the **MOST** of every moment.

You **ARE**
what you do
DAILY.

Most of the people you know will **NEVER** achieve success. They'll dream about it. They'll talk about it. But most of them won't possess it. Why is that? Because most people don't **UNDERSTAND** success. It isn't the lottery. Nor is it a place you find when you reach some magical time of life. Success is not a destination thing—it's a **DAILY** thing.

YOU CAN ACHIEVE IF YOU BELIEVE

*Trust in the LORD with all your heart,
and do not rely on your own understanding;
think about Him in all your ways,
and He will guide you on the right paths.*

PROVERBS 3:5-6

FOLLOWERS don't give their best to something they don't **UNDERSTAND**. Nobody becomes **MOTIVATED** by something he kinda, sorta believes in.

Never forget that you are a **MIRACLE**, that you are unique, possessing talents, experiences, and opportunities that no one else has ever had— or will ever have. It is your **RESPONSIBILITY** to become everything that you are.

One of the most common questions from people in leadership positions is, "How do I get a **VISION** for my organization?" That is a **CRUCIAL** question, because until it is answered, a person will be a leader in **NAME ONLY**.

Sadly, far too many people have dreams that are not **GENUINE**, but simply wishful thinking that fills their thoughts but will never **FULFILL** their lives.

Your **ATTITUDE**,
more than your aptitude,
will determine your
ALTITUDE.

There are no halfhearted **CHAMPIONS**.

SHALLOW men believe in luck.
STRONG men believe in
cause and effect.

The people who go far
do so because they
MOTIVATE themselves
and give life their **BEST**,
regardless of how
they **FEEL**.

You may **SUCCEED** if nobody else believes in you, but you will never succeed if you don't believe in **YOURSELF**.

PERSEVERE

I take pleasure in weakness, insults, catastrophes, persecutions, and in pressures, because of Christ. For when I am weak, then I am strong.

2 CORINTHIANS 12:10

The road to success is **UPHILL** all the way. Anyone who wants to **ACCOMPLISH** much must **SACRIFICE** much.

A leader's **COURAGE** is ultimately not for himself, but for all the people **DEPENDING** on him to lead.

DISAPPOINTMENT is the gap that exists between expectation and **REALITY**. All of us have encountered that gap. We've had to live with our unfulfilled desires and had our hopes dashed. Disappointments can be highly damaging to us. Novelist Mark Twain observed, "We should be careful to get out of an experience only the wisdom that is in it—and stop there; lest we be like the cat that sits down on a hot stove lid. She will never sit down on a hot stove lid again—and that is well. But also she will never sit down on a cold lid anymore."

Uncommon leaders are **FINALISTS**: They labor with **DILIGENCE** and **DEDICATION** to the end so that they finish well.

Noah was the first person to make great **SACRIFICES** to become a **LEADER**. How would you feel if you were required to give up every **PLACE** and every **PERSON** you had ever known (other than seven family members) to be the leader God wanted you to be? That's what Noah did.

Harriet Tubman would appear to be an unlikely candidate for **LEADERSHIP**, because the deck was certainly stacked against her. She was uneducated. She lived in a culture that didn't respect African Americans. And she labored in a country where women didn't even have the right to vote yet. **DESPITE HER CIRCUMSTANCES**, she became an incredible leader. John Brown, the famed revolutionary abolitionist, referred to her as "General Tubman" and was quoted as saying that she was "a better officer than most whom I have seen. She could command an army as successfully as she led her small parties of fugitives."

It takes **TIME** to become worthy of followers. Leadership isn't learned or earned in a **MOMENT**.

Our **MOTIVES** have as much to do with accomplishing our mission as do our gifts and talents. Bono, lead singer of U2, recalls a time when he and his bandmates asked, "Can we relax?" following their early commercial successes. In that moment, he pushed the group to continue its quest to be relevant.

He said, "If you're judging where we are by [what we can afford to buy], it's a dangerous measure. I judge where we are by how close I am to the melody I'm hearing in my head, and how close are we to what we can do as a band to realize our potential." U2's long-running influence has perhaps been driven as much by the group's **PASSIONATE DRIVE** to reach its potential as by its musical genius.

When times get **TOUGH**,
I encourage you to hear what
characters from the **BIBLE** would
say if they were to come down
from "the cloud of witnesses"
and run beside you.

People who have **GIVEN UP** are ruled by their darkest mistakes, worst failures, and deepest regrets. If you want to be **SUCCESSFUL**, then be governed by your finest thoughts, your highest enthusiasm, your greatest optimism, and your most **TRIUMPHANT** experiences.

One of the reasons leaders need courage and character is that **SACRIFICE** is often a crucial part of **LEADERSHIP**.

As a **COMMUNICATOR**, perhaps nothing is worse than scanning the audience halfway through a presentation, only to see people fiddling with smartphones, fidgeting in their chairs, or—worst of all—falling asleep in a puddle of drool. If someone had filmed my life, my communication blunders and mistakes could be turned into hours of **HUMOROUS OUTTAKES**. Learning to **CONNECT** with people has been an ongoing process for me, involving trial by error and plenty of disconnects. Yet I am grateful for my failures, for they have taught me **VALUABLE LESSONS** about getting through to others. Hopefully you can glean from my missteps as you hone your own skills as a connector.

Motivation gets you going, but **DISCIPLINE** keeps you **GROWING**. That's the Law of Consistency. It doesn't matter how talented you are. It doesn't matter how many opportunities you receive. If you want to grow, consistency is key.

In the most difficult of times, **COURAGE** is what makes someone a **LEADER**.

No one can be **GIVEN** the right to lead. The right to lead can only be **EARNED**. And that takes time.

The most important **VICTORY** is to conquer **SELF**. When we give up or let ourselves live in mediocrity, our leadership will never reach its **POTENTIAL**. However, being disciplined maximizes our abilities, our character, and, in addition to our talent, it will help us **WIN** the battle within.

Leadership is often **EASY** during the good times. It's when everything seems to be **AGAINST** you—when you're out of energy, and you don't want to lead—that you earn your place as a **LEADER**. During every season of life, leaders face crucial moments when they must choose between gearing up or giving up. To make it through those times, rely on the rock of **DISCIPLINE**, not the shifting sand of emotion.

WINNING WITH TEAMWORK

*Above all, put on love—
the perfect bond of unity.*

COLOSSIANS 3:14

No matter how **GOOD** you are, you will always miss some **DETAILS** when making decisions. Partner with people who see what you don't.

The truth is that **TEAMWORK** is at the heart of great **ACHIEVEMENT**. The question isn't whether teams have value. The question is whether we **ACKNOWLEDGE** that fact and become better team players. As leaders, we are called to cast vision for our teams, but also to get down in the trenches. In order to reach goals and achieve success, we must recognize the **IMPORTANCE** of the team.

As you consider your journey toward ever-greater leadership, you'll need **GOOD COMPANIONS**. Your inner circle will **MAKE YOU** or **BREAK YOU**.

Look around you—
what is happening to others?
As a leader, you must always take
into account **OTHER PEOPLE**.
If others aren't with you,
you aren't leading.

One of the **IRONIES** of leadership is that you become a better leader by **SHARING** whatever power you have, not by saving it all for yourself. You're meant to be a **RIVER**, not a reservoir. If you use your power to **EMPOWER** others, your leadership will **EXTEND** far beyond your grasp.

CONNECTING is all about others. However, as an inexperienced leader I wore myself out trying to get people to support what I wanted to accomplish. Eventually, I learned that instead of trying to conform others to my agenda, I should **POSITION MYSELF** to see things from their vantage point. As I gained **AWARENESS** of the needs and hopes of others, I was able to add **VALUE** to their lives in practical ways. I had to prove that I had their **BEST INTERESTS** in mind prior to earning their wholehearted commitment.

Leadership is by nature **RELATIONAL**. Today's generation of leaders seems particularly aware of this, because title and position mean so little to them. They know intuitively that people **GO ALONG** with people they **GET ALONG** with.

If you find yourself **STARVING** for success, one of the best ways to get things going in your life is to be around people who are **ACHIEVING** success. Spend time with them. Watch how they work. **LEARN** how they think. You will inevitably become like the people you are around.

Nothing of **SIGNIFICANCE** was ever achieved by an individual acting alone. Look below the surface and you will find that all seemingly solo acts are really **TEAM EFFORTS**. Have you ever met a successful person who has not had **SUPPORT** or **GUIDANCE** from another person? One of the most important factors to success is **TEAMWORK**. Without a team, leaders rely solely on themselves and their own skills. There's less room for growth, innovation, and collaboration.

People who cannot **GET ALONG** with others will **NEVER GET AHEAD** in life.

Remember, man does not live on **BREAD ALONE**. Sometimes he needs a little **BUTTERING UP**.

CHARACTER COUNTS

The fruit of the Spirit is love, joy, peace, patience, kindness, goodness, faith, gentleness, self-control. Against such things there is no law.

GALATIANS 5:22-23

INTEGRITY will take a leader farther than any other quality. If you would travel far and do much as a leader, **NEVER COMPROMISE** your integrity.

The highest reward for your work is not what you **GET** for it, but what you **BECOME** by it.

Your **CHARACTER** is your most effective means of **PERSUASION**.

COMMITMENT
in the face of **CONFLICT**
creates **CHARACTER**.

The **MEASURE** of your character is what you would do if you were sure **NO ONE** would ever find out.

Character protects your **TALENT**— and allows you to build upon what you already have. In order to protect our talent, we must **INVEST** in that which is hidden below the surface. Similar to an iceberg, there is more than meets the eye. Strong character allows talent to **HOLD UP** when storms come. Character creates a **FOUNDATION** upon which you can build your life. If there are cracks in that foundation, you cannot build much.

INTEGRITY is more than our talk. Integrity brings **SECURITY**. Integrity's absence leads to ruin.

To achieve **REAL SUCCESS**, you have to do it from the **INSIDE OUT**. Focus on your character, and your whole life improves. Changes in character bring **SUBSTANCE** and **POWER**, while external improvements are merely cosmetic and quickly fade away.

No matter how many **POSITIVE QUALITIES** a leader possesses, he cannot lead for long if he lacks **CHARACTER**. Without character, even the most talented leader's contribution to his followers will be **SHORT-REACHING**… and easily forgotten.

As a leader, you have to take **RESPONSIBILITY** for your own failures as well as successes. That's the only way you'll learn. If you keep **LEARNING**, you'll improve. If you improve, your **LEADERSHIP** will get better. And in time, you will earn the right to lead on the level you deserve.

Few things are more **DANGEROUS** than a leader with an **UNEXAMINED** life.

While your **CIRCUMSTANCES** are beyond your control, your **CHARACTER** is not.

Don't **HIDE** bad news.
With multiple information
channels available, bad news
always becomes **KNOWN**.
Be **CANDID** right from the start.

LEAD LONG, LEAD STRONG

A generous person will be blessed.

PROVERBS 22:9

Leaders **PROVIDE** for their people what the people cannot provide for themselves.

Rare is the effective leader who didn't learn to become a **GOOD FOLLOWER** first. West Point has produced more **LEADERS** than Harvard Business School.

Leaders don't get bogged down in the minutia. They see everything from the vantage point of the **MOUNTAINTOP**. That's why their goals are called **VISION**.

A good leader **ENLARGES** people. If you want a quick-and-easy test of your leadership, simply look around at your people and ask: "Are they **GROWING**?" As Alan Loy McGinnis said, "There is no more noble occupation in the world than to assist another human being—to help someone succeed." Leaders make their people better, helping them to go higher than they could have by themselves.

You've got to love your **PEOPLE** more than your **POSITION**.

No one respects and follows mediocrity. Leaders who earn the right to lead **GIVE THEIR ALL** to what they do. They bring into play not only their skills and talents, but also **GREAT PASSION** and **HARD WORK**. They perform at the **HIGHEST LEVEL** of which they are capable.

The key to becoming an **EFFECTIVE** leader is not to focus on making other people follow, but on making yourself the kind of person they **WANT** to follow. You must become someone that others can **TRUST** to take them where they want to go.

To **MEASURE** a leader, put a tape around his **HEART**, not his head.

When did you **FIRST REALIZE** that you were a leader? For me it happened as a fifth-grade student in Mr. Horton's classroom. We were studying the legal system, and we planned to assemble a mock courtroom with attorneys, a jury, and a judge. When it came time to elect the judge, Mr. Horton passed out ballots, and we wrote down the name of the student who we thought ought to be the judge...

...I voted for Bill Phillips, who lived down the street from me. Truthfully, I thought he'd be chosen as the judge. Yet, when we tallied up the votes of the twenty-seven kids in the class, twenty-six had voted for me, and my ballot was the only one for Bill. For the first time in my life, as a fifth-grader, I realized, "Oh, my goodness! **I'M A LEADER**."

A strong leader **NAVIGATES** for people. On whitewater raft trips, before travelers ever enter the water, the guide warns them of the dangers that lie ahead. During the voyage, before reaching particularly rough stretches, the guide pulls over to the riverbank and leads rafters uphill to show them upcoming rapids and whirlpools. That way, the rafters can see ahead of time the hazards they are going to encounter.

Leadership isn't about **POSITION**. Leadership is about using your **INFLUENCE** exactly where you are.

Some people lead
for a **LIFETIME**.
Others receive
only a **MOMENT**
to show the way.

INFLUENCE doesn't come to us instantaneously; it increases **GRADUALLY**. Nor does influence develop by accident. Instead, it grows as we **PURPOSEFULLY** take action to earn the trust and win the respect of others.

There are countless questions leaders can ask themselves to gauge their **GROWTH**. For example:

"How can I **IMPROVE**?"

"How can I gain **WISDOM**?"

"How can I improve **RELATIONSHIPS** with those around me?"

Each of these questions offers great insight into progress and growth. However, in order to move forward, leaders must apply the insight and be **INTENTIONAL** in bridging the gap between plans to grow and true growth.

Leaders take **RISKS**. That's not to say that they are reckless, because good leaders aren't. But they don't always take the **SAFEST ROUTE**. Rarely can a person **BREAK GROUND** and play it safe at the same time.

"What's my **MOTIVATION**?"
That's the question crossing our minds when the alarm goes off at six in the morning. That's the question we pose to ourselves at the office when the clock rolls past five p.m. and there is still work needing to be done. At some point, all leaders must consciously face the motive questions: "Why am I doing what I am doing? Why do I want to lead, really? Why do I desire **INFLUENCE**?" Experience has taught me that why we do something will ultimately determine what we do. **ACTION** flows from **INTENTION**. For this reason, it's imperative for us, as leaders, to regularly **EVALUATE** our primary motivations.

Leadership always has a **COST**. To be a leader, you may not be asked to leave your country or give up all your possessions, as Moses was. But you can be sure that leading others will have a **PRICE**.

Teams need 360-Degree Leaders. These are the type of leaders who lead **UP** (to the boss), **ACROSS** (among peers), and **DOWN** (to others). A 360-Degree Leader leads through **INFLUENCE**, not position, power, or leverage. Oftentimes, they face the myth that they can't lead unless they are at the top of the totem pole. However, we can better our organizations and help fulfill a **GRANDER VISION** by serving as 360-Degree Leaders.

We commonly think of a leader's greatest **VICTORY** as being over others, as defeating an opposing team or a rival business. However, as Plato wrote, "The first and best victory is to conquer self." Every leader faces a struggle against **SELF-INTERESTEDNESS**. Yet whereas followers tend to think of themselves first, leaders have learned to put **OTHERS** ahead of themselves.

INTEGRITY is the **ONE THING** a leader cannot do without.

Leadership always requires **COURAGE**. In fact the word "courage" comes from the French word *couer,* meaning heart. A leader must have the **HEART** to communicate his vision, no matter how absurd it may sound to others, to risk defeat in the face of bitter odds, to put himself and his reputation on the line, and to **REACH OUT** to others in order to take them on the journey.

In the end, **WHERE** you lead and **WHO** you lead are less important than **HOW** you lead.

"What is the one thing I really need to know about **LEADERSHIP**?" I've heard this question dozens of times from people eager to be influential, but impatient with the slow road of diligent study and personal growth. My response never quite seems to satisfy them: "The one thing you need to know to become a great leader is that there's **MORE THAN ONE THING** you need to know about leadership!"

Leaders who last...

Develop personal **DISCIPLINE**.

Put their confidence in **GOD**.

Keep the **VALUE** of material possessions in **PERSPECTIVE**.

Recognize the **DANGER** of becoming a slave to **PLEASURE**.

Seek and refresh **GOD'S VISION** for their lives.

JOHN MAXWELL'S QUOTABLE QUIPS

*Who is like the wise person, and who
knows the interpretation of a matter?
A man's wisdom brightens his face.*

ECCLESIASTES 8:1

Leadership is developed **DAILY**, but not in a **DAY**.

Believing in people **BEFORE** they have proved themselves is the key to **MOTIVATING** people to reach their **POTENTIAL**.

The greatest **MISTAKE** we make is living in constant **FEAR** that we will make a mistake!

A difficult time can be more **READILY ENDURED** if we retain the conviction that our **EXISTENCE** holds a **PURPOSE**, a cause to pursue, a person to love, and a goal to **ACHIEVE**.

If you keep doing what you've **ALWAYS DONE**, you'll always get what you've **ALWAYS GOTTEN**.

A leader **KNOWS** the way, **GOES** the way, and **SHOWS** the way.

When there is no **HOPE** in the future, there is no **POWER** in the present.

The Law of Awareness says you must "know yourself to grow yourself." What that means is that in order to achieve **GROWTH**, leaders must hone in on **WHO** they are and **WHAT** they desire to do.

Let go of your **EGO**. The truly great leaders are not in leadership for **PERSONAL GAIN**. They lead in order to **SERVE** other people.

John Wooden was a man of hall-of-fame **CHARACTER** long before he was a hall-of-fame **COACH**.

Every leader's vision is based on his or her own **PERSONAL EXPERIENCE**. What does your past tell you about your future?

We've all heard, "**EXPERIENCE** is the best teacher," but it's simply **NOT TRUE**. Experience is not the best teacher; it never has been and never will be. **MATURITY** doesn't always come with time. Sometimes **AGE** brings nothing more than **WRINKLES** and **GRAY HAIR**.

A **PROBLEM** is something that can be **SOLVED**. A **FACT OF LIFE** is something that must be **ACCEPTED**.

When you look at the **LEADERS** whose names are revered long after they have finished leading, you find that they were men and women who helped people to live **BETTER LIVES** and reach their **POTENTIAL**.

You can't be a

SMART COOKIE

if you have a

CRUMMY ATTITUDE.

If a person doesn't govern his **TEMPER**, his temper will govern **HIM**.

A **WINNER** is big enough to **ADMIT** his mistakes, smart enough to **PROFIT** from them, and strong enough to **CORRECT** them.

There's never enough time to do **EVERYTHING**, but there's always enough time to do the **MOST IMPORTANT** thing.

A great leader's
COURAGE to fulfill his vision
comes from **PASSION**,
not **POSITION**.

For **TEAMS** to develop at every level, they need **LEADERS** at every level.

GROWTH doesn't just happen. Growth is **INTENTIONAL**. Each of us has the opportunity to choose growth or to be complacent with where we stand.

Leadership is important no matter **WHO** you are or **WHERE** you lead. And even in a pack of dogs, the one who stays in front has to **EARN** the right to lead.

Self-discipline is the **ABILITY** to do what is **RIGHT** even when you don't **FEEL** like doing it.

Everything **RISES** and **FALLS** on leadership.

Young people live in the **FUTURE**.
Old people live in the **PAST**.
Wise people live in the **PRESENT**.

*May you be blessed by the Lord,
the Maker of heaven and earth.*

PSALM 115:15

Humble yourselves, therefore,
under the mighty hand of God,
so that He may exalt you
at the proper time.

1 PETER 5:6